First published 2010 by
Veritas Publications
7–8 Lower Abbey Street
Dublin 1
Ireland
publications@veritas.ie
www.veritas.ie

ISBN 978 1 84730 224 3

A catalogue record for this book is available from the British Library.

Designed by Kelly Sheridan, Outsource Graphix Ltd, Dublin
Printed in the Republic of Ireland by Walsh Colour Print, Kerry

Veritas books are printed on paper made from the wood pulp of managed forests. For every tree felled, at least one tree is planted, thereby renewing natural resources.

D0486691

P/2175850

About the Authors

Fiona McAuslan holds a Masters in Mediation and Conflict Resolution Studies from University College Dublin. She is an experienced mediator and conflict coach with many years' experience working with family, workplace and school conflicts. She works in the Irish Family Mediation Service and Clanwilliam Institute and is an accredited Practitioner Mediator with the Mediators Institute of Ireland. Fiona has published the S.A.L.T. Programme: A Conflict Resolution Education Programme for Primary schools. She lives in North County Dublin with her husband, Michael, and two children, Sarah and Ben.

Peter Nicholson is a communications specialist and has built a very successful Marketing and Visual Communications Business over the last fifteen years. Peter and Fiona met whilst working on the S.A.L.T. programme and they have continued to work together on many other projects. He is married to Karen, and they have two children, Patrick and Ailish.

About the Illustrator

Kelly Sheridan studied Classical and Computer Animation in Ballyfermot College of Further Education for three years before attending the Irish Academy of Computer Training (IACT) to study Graphic Design and Desktop Publishing. A keen illustrator and life drawer, she loves the work of Tim Burton and Walter Sickert. Originally from Crumlin, Kelly currently lives in Tallaght with her partner, Mark.

Read Me First!

This is not just another story book, it's a Tool Book. So what's a Tool Book then? It's a book that explains an issue, shows how children can be affected by it and how they can resolve the problem. It also offers a number of tips and techniques that can be used again and again to improve the ability to deal with Sibling Rivalry on a day-to-day basis.

Section 1
What is Sibling Rivalry?
This is a simple explanation of what Sibling Rivalry is.

Section 2
The Story
The story helps the reader identify Sibling Rivalry in their world and helps open the door to discussing and resolving the issue.

Section 3
Tool Box
The Tool Box has many tips and techniques that can be used in everyday life on an ongoing basis. The more they are practised, the better the result!

What is Sibling Rivalry?

• Sibling Rivalry is the natural competition that happens between brothers and sisters.

• Falling out or having rows with each other is part of life for siblings.

• The word for these rows or fights is 'conflict'.

• When we argue over who is going to do the dishes or whose turn it is to choose the TV channel, we are 'in conflict'.

• There are many types of conflict, big and small. They are a part of life.

NOT ALL CONFLICT IS BAD. We can use our disagreements to find better solutions.

How Does Conflict Happen?

• One person says or does something that annoys the other person.

• The other person retaliates.

• More hurtful things are said and each person starts feeling annoyed and upset.

• The more annoyed and upset each person gets, the more they say things to hurt the other.

• It gets harder for each of them to talk about what they really mean.

• Sometimes other people get involved, which can make the problem bigger.

More info VISIT www.resolvingbooks.com/howconflicthappens

Brothers and Sisters

Brothers and sisters not only live together, they have to share a lot of things, like their Mum and Dad, the bathroom, toys. They know all the good things and bad things about each other. It can be hard to share toys, or your room, or Mum and Dad.

Have you ever seen baby birds when their mum comes back with food? They all want to be fed first. They fight to get the food. Humans have this instinct too. We compete with each other in families to get our parents' attention.

Brothers and sisters share a deep family bond but still compete with each other at the same time. It is natural for disagreement to happen.

I Hate You / I Like You

When we are young we can find it hard to understand our feelings.

It is easy to confuse 'I like you' with 'I hate you'! It is called an 'interaction error'!

Playing and arguing helps us learn to be 'social experts'.

I like you

I hate you

I hate you

More info VISIT www.resolvingbooks.com/siblingsemotions

I want to
watch
the TV
alone

**Let's watch
together**

**Let's watch
together**

Leave me
alone

Let's play

Let's play

Let's share

It's mine

It's mine

What is Sibling Rivalry?

11

What Do We Learn When We Argue?

When we row with others we learn about ourselves and our siblings.

We learn:
- to negotiate power struggles.
- to find better solutions.
- to say sorry.
- to forgive and forget.

Just because you're older, doesn't mean you're right!

Your Brain's Internet

Our brains are connected with each other just like computers are connected on the internet. Feelings can spread from mind to mind without us being aware.

When we feel annoyed, it can spiral into an argument.

Sometimes, what we argue about can seem small but feel big.

We do as they do, and then the

More info VISIT www.resolvingbooks.com/brainsinternet

as we do, and then we do as they do, and then they do as we do, and then we do as they do, and then we do as they do, and then they do as we do, and then we do as they do, and then they do as we do, and then we do as they do, and then we do as they do, and then they do as we do, and then they do as we do, and then we do as they do, and then they do as we do, and then we do as they do, and then they do as we do, and then they do as we do, and then we do as they do, and then we do as they do, and then they do as we do, and then we do, and then we do as they do, and then we do as they do, and then we do as they do, and then they do as we do, and then we do as they do, and then they do as we do, and then we do, and then they do as we do, and then they do as we do, and then we do as they do, and then we do, and then they do as we do, and then we do, and then we do, and then we do as they do, and then they do as we do, and then they do as we do, and then we do as they do, and then we do as they do, and then they do as we do, and then we do, and then they do as we do, and then we do as they do, and then they do as we do, and then they do as we do

What is Sibling Rivalry?

15

Lynsey and Gary are brother and sister.

Lynsey and Gary walk to school together.
They play games with their friends and
spend lots of time with each other.

The Story

One of their favourite games is basketball. Their friends always join them after school to play a game with them.

After they leave, Lynsey and Gary often talk about their day.

They annoyed each other.

Sometimes they argued when they played with others.

They usually sorted it out, somehow.

One afternoon, Lynsey and Gary started arguing.
This was happening a lot lately.

They kept shouting and shouting...
even after everyone else had stopped playing.
Their friends were so fed up!

P/2175850

It wasn't only their
friends who got fed up...

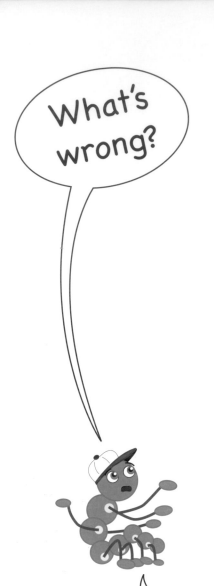

When we argue we forget what else matters.
It is hard to remember we are friends.

On the TV, Lynsey and Gary were arguing. Gary called Lynsey a cheater and Lynsey called Gary a liar.

Their friends were upset, annoyed and fed up with them.

You each get angrier and angrier with each other.

You say things that hurt each other.

You start to feel upset.

It gets harder for each of you to talk about how you really feel and what you really think.

This is what is happening to you.

Lynsey was really mad.

Why did she do that? Maybe I should ask?

I'll try. Here goes...

8
7
6
5
4
3
2
1

LISTEN AND TALK

Well, we can't both be right.

What do we do?

WHAT WOULD BE A FAIR SOLUTION?

Maybe we should take the shot again?

Or ask the others what they saw?

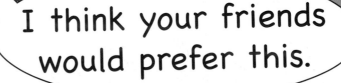

I think your friends would prefer this.

Talking Together

1. Pick a time when it is possible to talk without interruptions.

2. Sit somewhere comfortable.

3. Do not answer the phone if possible.

4. Remember the power of listening. You do not need to have all the answers.

5. Use open questions: What, Who, Where, How?

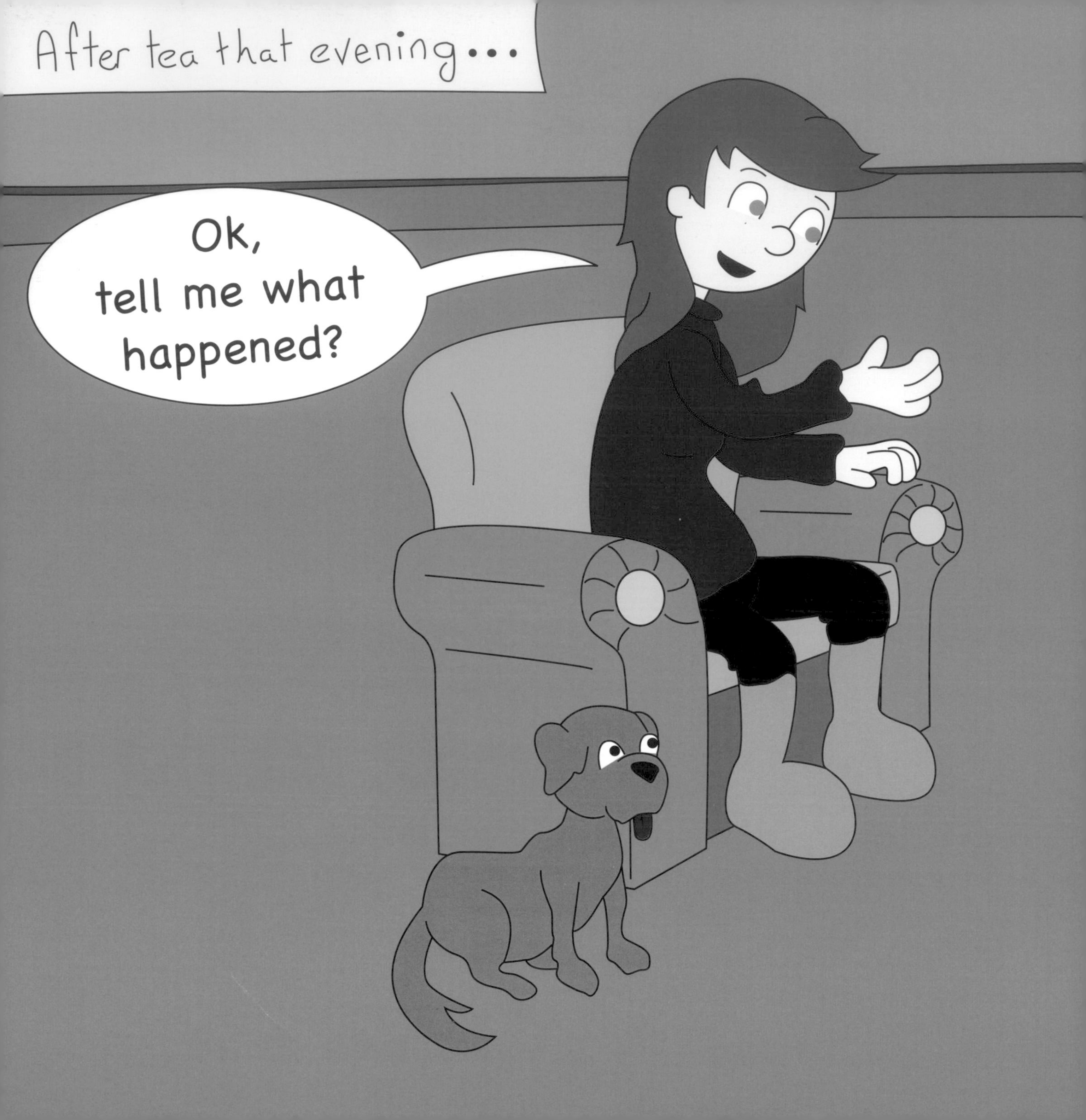
After tea that evening...
Ok, tell me what happened?

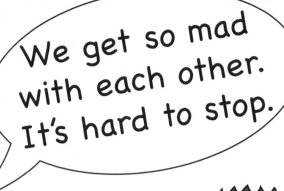

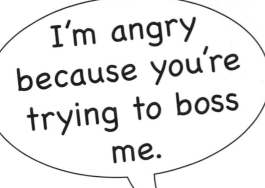

The Caterpillar

- The Caterpillar in the story plays the part of a mediator. The questions he asks and the way he listens are all done using mediation skills.

- A mediator does not judge people or take sides. Their role is to use their skills to help people resolve their own conflict. They do this by listening to each person, asking questions and using negotiation techniques to help the person think and learn about what they are feeling.

- The mediator helps them to talk to each other and to understand each other's point of view. In doing so, they can find a way forward together.

Stays Cool

Helps Find Solutions

Understands

Remains Impartial

Asks Good Questions

Doesn't Judge

Tool Box

The Caterpillar Helped Because...

Listening helps calm kids.

Listening helps kids work things out for themselves.

Good questions help kids talk about what really bothers them.

Focusing on them helps kids think about their own thoughts and feelings.

Helping kids sort it out for themselves helps them learn to be better friends.

Skills used by the Caterpillar in this story:

1. **Listening** to what Lynsey and Gary felt and why they got angry with each other is a more effective way of helping them learn from their row. If they were simply told to behave, they would not have had the opportunity to learn about what made them angry and how to handle this emotion better in the future.

2. The **questions** the Caterpillar asks help Lynsey and Gary talk about what really bothers them and makes a big difference in how they understand the real nature of their row.

3. The Caterpillar does not talk about himself. **He concentrates on Lynsey and Gary.** This means they have to focus on their own thoughts and feelings.

4. The Caterpillar **does not sort out the problem. He leaves that to the siblings**, who at the end of the day learn more from doing it their way. They learn how to be better friends.

All the skills and ideas that the Caterpillar uses can be used by anyone reading this story to help them in their own lives.

Use Words

We all get annoyed with each other. It's like a switch going on. We need to find out what 'flicks the switch'. We do that by talking, not fighting.

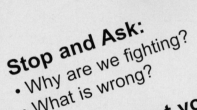

Stop and Ask:
- Why are we fighting?
- What is wrong?

Listen to what you are both saying.

Talk about what is really upsetting you both.

Conflict Iceberg

What we
can see

What we
can't see

Remember that we don't always know what is really wrong with the other person. It is like looking at an iceberg and only seeing the tip.

We need to look below the water to find out the real story. We do that by listening and talking.

Here are some good questions to ask to help someone talk about how they really feel:

1. What happened?

2. What did you do?

3. What do you think about what happened?

4. How did you feel?

5. How are you now?

6. What do you think should happen next?

7. What do you want to do?

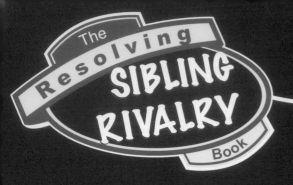
Listen and Talk

When we shout at each other our heads get hotter and hotter.

We can't think straight and winning matters more than friendship.

Afterwards we feel sad and lost.

We don't know what to do.

We feel lonely and confused.

We feel hurt and angry all at the same time and we need to win.

Listening calms us down.

Listening finds better solutions.

We both win if we listen to each other.

Listening helps us feel better.

Powerful Questions

Asking questions can help us learn what is wrong. It can help the other person talk. Asking questions helps us resolve our arguments.

A powerful question is a question that can help somebody think through a situation and figure out what to do.

There are many good questions. Here are some:

✔ **1. What has happened?**

✔ **2. What is wrong?**

✔ **3. What did you do?**

✔ **4. What did I do that upset you?**

✔ **5. Are you alright?**

✔ **6. What do you want to do now?**

Circuit Breaker

1, 2, 3

1, 2, 3

Three big breaths is all it takes to break the circuit.

Remember:

1. Take three big breaths.

2. Count backwards from ten.

3. Think about what you want to say.

4. Start with 'I feel...' or 'I think...'.

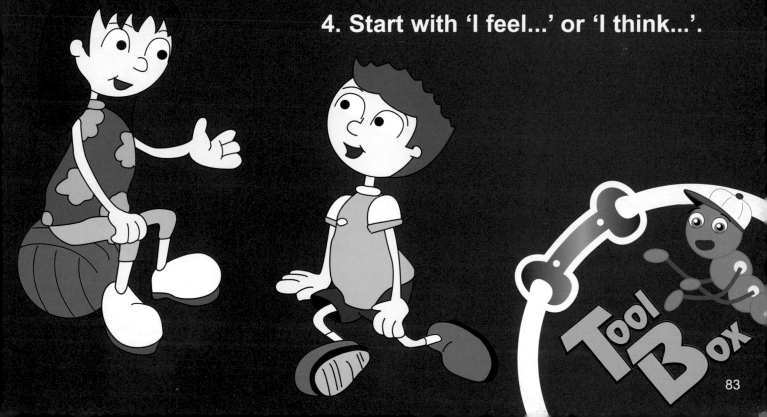

Tool Box

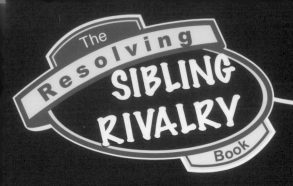

A Talking Corner Can Be A Good Idea

The things we fight about do not cause the conflict. In fact they can help resolve it if we know how to talk about it and how to listen.

The solution to the row can only come when you have listened to each other and understand how you both feel.

STOP
LISTEN
TALK

How to talk:

1. Find a comfortable place to talk.

2. Talk honestly but not hurtfully.

3. Listen to the other person's point of view.

4. Try to find a way forward that works for both of you.

Be Positive About Conflict

Learning to be Conflict Positive

It can take time to change how you fight. There will be times when it goes wrong. It is possible to learn from these times.

Thinking about what happened can help us learn for the future. It is never too late to talk about what happened.

What we do next time:

1. Notice when we are beginning to get angry.

2. Take three big breaths and count backwards from ten.

3. Ask powerful questions. Remember, a powerful question is a question that can help somebody to think through the situation and figure out what to do.

4. Talk honestly but not hurtfully.

5. Try to find a way forward that works for both of you.

Rehearsal Room

Tool Box

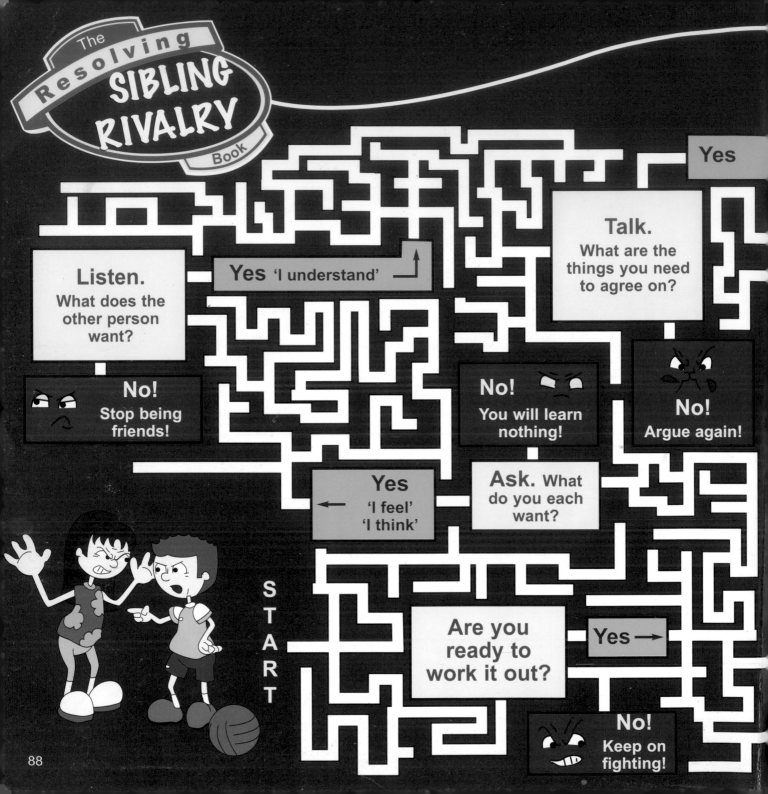